MEN
AND MODELS

IAN MARCHANT

MEN
AND MODELS

CONTENTS

MEN AND MODELS:
INSTRUCTIONS AND PAINTING GUIDE

I remember as a child, aged perhaps eight or nine, being taken by my grandmother to visit an elderly neighbour of hers – a kindly old countryman with nut brown skin, twinkling blue eyes, and the strong hands of a craftsman. I was taken to visit this paragon (I can no longer remember his name) because he made beautiful models of gypsy caravans from used matchsticks. Around the walls was ranged a matchwood caravanserai: brightly painted bowtops, elegant Reading wagons and gaudy showman's vans.

Sitting in the old man's sunlit parlour that afternoon, surrounded by the fruit of a lifetime's work, I thought to myself, 'Stupid old fool. Why on earth would anybody go to all the bother of sticking together hundreds of matchsticks, when you could just get a nice kit at the toyshop for two-and-six?'

He died a few months after our meeting, just as the new money came in, from a smoking-related illness.

How naïve I was. Plastic construction kits, which were what lads of my generation thought of as 'models', were, in fact, a very new phenomenon. Older people, if they wanted to make models, didn't have kits, they had matchsticks, or lollipop sticks, or cardboard and balsa. They had tissue paper and flour and water. Above all, they had skill and patience. Growing up in the '60s and '70s, we had neither. We had Airfix.

Airfix was founded in 1939, and they specialised in making combs: by 1947 they were the largest manufacturer of plastic combs in Britain. That had been their contribution to the war effort: seeing that the Brylcreme Boys in the RAF had combs to keep their hair in order. It was the beginning of a long and fruitful relationship with the Few. And, to be frank, with the Luftwaffe. The first aircraft kit was a Spitfire, released in 1953, but you had to have baddies, so German planes followed shortly after. The German role in contemporary modelling cannot be over-emphasised. The first real model railways, for example, were made in Germany from about 1860 onwards.

BEFORE COMMENCING REMOVE ALL PIECES FROM THE SPRULE

Me and my pals would buy a Spitfire, or a Heinkel bomber, wrench the bits from the sprule and glue the bits crudely together. We would always make sure that we made them with the undercarriage tucked away, as it's much easier to do. This left you with the wheels, which were simply discarded, along with the sprule. Our painting technique was crude, too. Some paint would usually get on the carpet. Then our mums would say something crude and chase us out of the house and down the street.

You did the transfers by soaking the sheet of RAF roundels or German crosses in a saucer. They floated away from the backing paper, and then you fished them out, and stuck them on the side of your aeroplane, in the wrong place, where they crinkled up like a baby's foreskin. The best thing about making these kits was putting drops of the glue on polystyrene, which melted and went sticky. This was a good thing. When we finished the kits, we set fire to them and lobbed them at our toy soldiers.

We were not modellers. We were playing. This was naughty. Proper modellers are not playing because proper models are not toys. Proper modellers paint all the bits before they start gluing. In fact, this might serve as a useful distinction between proper modellers and kids playing with construction kits: modellers paint the bits that you can't see when the model is completed, such as the pilot's feet.

We never painted the pilot at all, since he was soon to die in a horrible inferno of melting plastic, and there seemed little point.

A modeller is someone who seeks to reflect reality, which he calls the prototype. Proper modelling is a serious business. Science proceeds by constructing models, which it compares with reality. If the model looks a bit like the prototype, then scientists are happy and can build another model. They use hard sums to build their models from, and almost never plastic kits – except Watson and Crick, who did use plastic kits to model DNA. That's all right, though, because they used hard sums later.

9

WHY DO THEY DO WHAT THEY DO?

Hobby modellers do it for a hobby, but that's serious too. Sometimes, for a man, who, unlike the far superior female, has limited emotional equipment, hobbies can assume great importance.

I worked with a model collector for a time. He spent all his time at work visiting model aeroplane and car sites on the internet. (All my other colleagues visited other websites, where I suppose they also looked at pictures of models.) Every argument with his girlfriend sent him scurrying for the model shop – making these models calmed him down. Unfortunately, it enraged his girlfriend, as the models were very expensive, and took weeks to make, so he never had any money or free time left for her. This inevitably caused arguments, which was a shame.

Models don't answer back, and they have a black-and-white solution. There is a perfect end-state. Men like that. Emotion is much more elusive. It makes a much worse mess than dried-up glue.

THE GLUE THAT BINDS US TOGETHER

To do what you love, for it's own sake, is something close to happiness. Modellers model for love, for their own satisfaction.

Some of the modellers featured in this book do build from kits. Others use wood and metal and paper and glue, and start from scratch. The thing that all the modellers have in common is the love that goes into their work, and the shared sense that they are trying to create something as close to perfection as they can achieve. Often, the making of the model becomes more important than the end result. I enjoyed talking to all of them very much, because of their love for what they do, and I thank them all for taking time out to share that love with me.

And, in a world full of cares and woes, famine and pestilence and war, isn't it reassuring to know that boating ponds still exist?

Ian Marchant

DEREK'S WINGÉD CHARIOT

Bleriot crossed the Channel, Lindburgh, the Atlantic, and Derek here aims to be the first man to fly a model aeroplane coast-to-coast across the narrowest part of England, west to east from Morecambe to Peterlee. That's 100 miles. Flying at around 40mph, you're talking two and a half hours in the air.

But how will Derek stay in touch with his plane, the 'Calliope'? Don't you have to keep radio-controlled things in sight? 'Ah, well. I was thinking of driving behind it in an open-topped car, but then I thought the police wouldn't be too chuffed. So now I'm going to fly after it in a microlite plane.' Have you found a pilot willing to take you? 'Oh yes. But model aircraft can't fly above 400 feet. And microlites aren't allowed to fly at less than 1,000... We'll think of something.'

And when you get there? 'I'll deliver a letter from the postmaster at Morecambe to the postmaster at Peterlee. Then I'll refuel, have a drink of whiskey, and fly back.'

12

"We shall overcome."

13

THE ENGLISH MINIATURIST

England is like the world in miniature, and the English have always loved this most intricate of art forms. Here's Cliff, the heir to a long line of miniaturists. His miniature model of a pub interior is like a Beryl Cook painting in 3D. 'I love pub interiors,' says Cliff. 'Odd, really, as I'm a teetotaller.' And his jewellers' workshop is painstakingly built inside a 1930s clock case. It took three months. You need steady hands, sharp eyes and an English imagination.

He started when his mother-in-law asked for a doll's house. Lesser men might not have risen to the challenge, but Cliff thought it was worth giving it a try and discovered in the process that he was an artist.

'I only build what pleases me,' he says, the proud mark of the true craftsman down the ages. 'There's a lot of poetic licence in these things.' You can see that. You can see the love squeezed into a small space. Maybe we should all listen more to our mothers-in-law.

"It brings out the best in people."

MINE IS MUCH BIGGER THAN YOURS

Phwoar! Look at this! Who needs Naomi Campbell? Kate Moss? This is a beauty, a thing of wonder, 30 feet long and 12 feet wide. All red-blooded men dream of having something like this in the attic. Gordon started building it eight years ago with his son, but luckily, his son lost interest pretty quickly, and Gordon could make it how he wanted. It's still far from finished (except for the viaduct) so it keeps growing and becoming more detailed.

The prototype is somewhere on The Great Western Railway, sometime just before nationalisation in 1947. To the railway modeller, this is when the railway was best, at its most romantic. But how do you get the space to build something so fantastic, and, frankly, big? 'Ah. We live in a bungalow. When I built the extension, I said to the wife, we could have our bedroom up here. She said, "Not likely. I don't want to go upstairs to bed." So I put the railway in here. Actually, I always knew she wouldn't want to sleep up here.' Clever man. Lucky, clever man.

"We needn't worry about the modern world any more."

HEAVENLY TOWERS

Here we have two models of a model. The prototype is in Paris: it was built by Monsieur Eiffel. The good people of Blackpool, seeing the prototype, wanted a model of it, and built one – the biggest model in the world. Then, after the war, Albert saw the model in Blackpool and said to himself, 'I could build a model of that.' But life got in the way. Besides, Albert wanted to build other things. A dab hand on the organ, Albert built his own. Then there was his pilot's licence to get. Oh, and the day job as a church minister.

On retirement, the ambition to model the Blackpool Tower came back. 'It put my geometry to the test, copying parabolic curves.' He started with Meccano, but Meccano is not to scale. So, with failing eyesight and the help of his nephew, he built the elegant curve of his own tower, from steel and aluminium, 5ft 2in high, 1:100 scale exactly. There are better models of the tower, Albert says. 'Mine is not the last word. There are some experts about the country.' Maybe. But how many of them could give a sermon, play the organ and fly a plane?

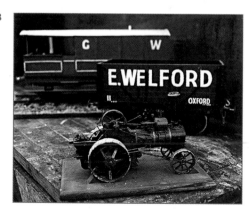

"Don't show off. If you're an expert, you don't need to."

'I'VE NEVER BOUGHT A BOX OF MATCHES'

So how did The Matchstick Fleet of more than 250 warships come to be built? 'People save them for me.'

In the world of marine modelling, The Matchstick Fleet is famous. Philip is the Daddy of matchstick modellers. People would be proud to have a matchstick of theirs in one of Philip's fanatically detailed models. The rotors on the helicopters rotate. The guns elevate on the revolving gun turrets. People wonder at the intricate drills and cutting equipment that Philip must have tucked away. 'I use razor blades, a straight edge, sandpaper and a hat-pin…' And 50 years of experience.

Philip has constructed a history of the post-war warship, in 1:300 scale, 1mm to every foot. His main weapon is patience, infinite patience. 'People who do this kind of thing tend to be the placid type – only happy and relaxed people would have the patience to fiddle about like this. You can't lose your temper can you? Matchstick modellers can't afford to flare up.' Just as well.

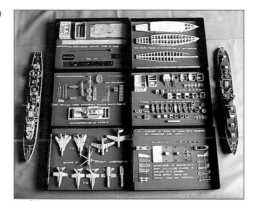

"I take enormous pleasure in meeting old sailors."

A QUESTION OF SCALE

Right. Scale. Interesting stuff. See the dome of the observatory in the background? Imagine the sun is that size. All the planets here are built by Ian to that scale. So Pluto, the furthest planet from the sun/dome is 4mm in diameter. That's how much bigger the sun is than Pluto. But, now, what if the distances between the models were to scale? Then Pluto would be 11km away from the dome. 'The photographer couldn't really get that in,' says Ian.

Ian paints all the surface details of the planets on to his models: fairly easy on the gas giants, trickier on Earth. They are used in the school where he works to show the lads the vastness of the universe. Imagine trying to find something 4mm across, 11km away, that kind of thing.

'They're can't be many people who've made a model of the Solar System,' says Ian. God, maybe? And the telescope, the ½-m reflecting telescope? Ian built that too.

"I make my models for me."

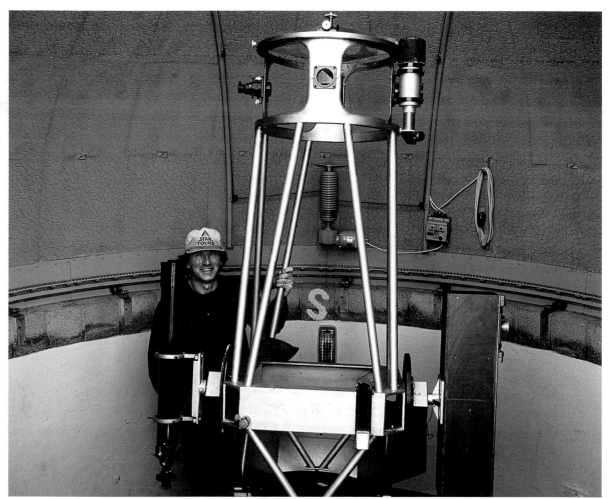

23

SEATED ONE DAY AT THE TINY ORGAN

Alan is a craftsman, who spent his working life with the Coal Board as a joiner, and also earned half a crown a picture as a photo-journalist on the side. Yet he always had time to make beautiful things, furniture in particular: 'Not so much models as the real thing.'

A life-long organ nutcase, he visited the Mecca of the Wurlitzer, the Blackpool Tower Ballroom, and saw a model of the mighty instrument, a model which didn't begin to do justice to the prototype. So, encouraged by his wife, Alan made a model of his own, which he presented to the Tower on completion. You can see it in the bar there for yourself, next time you're passing. He was so encouraged by the result, that he made two more models.

I guess they are disappearing, the Mighty Wurlitzer organs? 'No, not at all. They get preserved. By Organ Preservation Societies.' May Alan, and his tiny organs, be preserved.

"I played the Wurlitzer for ten minutes."

A BUSMAN'S HOLIDAY

...is spent scouring the globe for new models to add to the 8,300 that Geoff already owns – the world's largest bus collection. Geoff has had to move house three times to accommodate it. 'My wife and I, we travel to lots of different countries, like Turkey and India, looking for buses. You just don't know what's been produced until you look.' The smallest ones are ⅛ inch long. Architects use them in models to show where people will stand in the freezing rain outside offices and shopping centres waiting for buses... Then four tiny buses come along at once.

The biggest buses, though, are the 13 examples of the work of the legendary Ernie Johnson, built in Brighton between 1945 and 1958, and sold to all the great English seaside resorts for kiddies to play on. In Skegness, in Mablethorpe, in Morecambe, summers were nothing without a ride in one of Ernie's buses. Now they sit in Geoff's garage. 'They are much too valuable to let children clamber over them,' he says. Poor old Ernie would be turning in his grave.

"When I got married, I already had 380."

ALL QUIET ON THE WESTERN FRONT

When Steve wants a bit of peace and quiet, he moseys on down to The Dude Ranch he has built at the bottom of his garden. He drinks in the saloon, shops in the general store, and locks up baddies in the jailhouse. At night, he sits with his best girl by the campfire, eating chilli and listening to some good ole boy music from Tennessee. Yep, things are mighty peaceful in Stephen's little piece of the Old Wild West. 'I put my gear on when I go down there,' he says. 'Once you're down The Dude Ranch, it's absolutely quiet.'

Stephen would like to get out to see the real West for himself, but he can't, because he's frightened of flying, so he built his Western town from old photographs and sketches. He's almost out of room, but there's space for just one more building – a bunkhouse – so his friends don't have to sleep in the jailhouse no more... Or under the Boardwalk.

Yes sir, Stephen is a fine example of that great Western stereotype, The English Eccentric.

"I've never upset nobody..."

MALCOLM AND LUCINDA

Malcolm noticed that at a lot of model boat shows, there wasn't anything for the really little kids, so he thought he would build them a friendly dragon. Hence Lucinda, made from plywood and fibreglass with a mop for her hair. She swims around the boating lake and, as she swims, her eyes cross and she laughs. Malcolm has an audio link to Lucinda so that she can talk with the tinies. 'The kids love it, cos they can't see where the voice is coming from.'

The kids named her, too. Malcolm took her to a model exhibition and got the children who came along to have a look and write their idea for a name on a piece of paper. Lucinda was the clear winner.

She also squirts water from her mouth on to the kids. 'She carries her own water in a tank, water from the tap. She used to squirt pond water, but you can't now because of these EU laws.' Typical eurocrats. Coming over here and interfering with the good old-fashioned British pond water squirting radio-controlled dragon.

"She's modelled after the wife. When she was much younger."

FULL PLASTIC JACKET

Brian says that the kind of toy soldiers people like is a generational thing. The older collectors tend to like the metal model soldiers, whereas people in their 30s and 40s like the plastic ones. It's all to do with what you played with as a kid.

I had the little plastic ones, but we used to set fire to them and stuff. 'That's a shame. Some of them are worth a fortune,' says Brian. Do you play with them? 'Sometimes. Not a lot. H. G. Wells wrote a book, before WW1, called "Little Wars", setting out rules for playing with toy soldiers. I use those, occasionally.'

Brian's passion is converting the commercial plastic soldiers into mini-works of art. 'It means there's no particular model that I'm trying to hunt down, because whatever I want, I can make myself.' To do that, you have to melt them, don't you? Go on Brian – set them up, run them over with your train set, and torch them. It's great fun!

"It's peculiarly English."

IT'S LIFE, JIM...

I'm worried that Chris is standing on the wrong side of his con-ops console. Everybody knows that whoever starts an episode of Star Trek on the right-hand side of this desk will die horribly by the episode's end. Chris tells me that this is known in the world of Trekkies as 'red-shirt syndrome'. Chris has some sympathy for the Engineering Department, who traditionally wore the red shirts. 'I look more like a Scotty than a Riker,' he admits.

A long-term modeller of Star Trek subjects, Chris says the excitement is in the accurizing. You get the basic kit, and then you customize it, so that it looks as close to the original as possible. To accurize: to make something more accurate. It's a verb, but it's not in the dictionary, so I'm hoping for an attribution.

The con-ops desk is full size, but there isn't really such a thing as the Starship Enterprise, so it is difficult to say for sure how accurate the reconstruction is. It looks pretty convincing to me. A fine piece of accurization.

"There's blood, sweat and tear stains inside."

AS YOU'LL APPRECIATE, THIS IS NOT A TOY

At £800 apiece, you can see what Keith means. With petrol engines and speeds of up to 50mph over tarmac, Nitro Truck Racing is the Formula One of the radio-controlled racing world.

'It's an art,' says Keith, and he should know. He was third in the US Championship B final in Los Angeles, and he got through to the quarter-finals in a recent championship staged by the *Men and Motors* television channel. The races are timed by computers, and all the trucks contain transponders so that their qualifying times can be judged to the nearest hundredth of a second. The tracking of each truck can be adjusted to the smallest tolerances, and by adding oils with varying viscosity, the camberizing differential compressors can rejiggimify the prophandler. Then, by resequencing the transpondent coils on the transmittulator...

I've gone native, haven't I? I don't know what I'm on about, do I? Help me. Somebody help me...

"Not only does that apply to the front-end, it applies to the rear-end as well..."

A TALE OF TWO MODELS

…4,000 years apart. The first one is Stonehenge. Len built that because he had some bits of stone, which his wife said looked 'like Stonehenge'. Len agreed and put them together. His henge is ¹⁄₁₀-scale – about the same as the one featured in the Spinal Tap movie.

Then, a stroke of luck: Len had a pick-up on the National Lottery – not a big one, not a life changing amount, but enough to build his own Millennium Dome. After all, the big one was built using lottery money, too, Len reasoned, and, if Stonehenge was built about 2,000BC and the Dome 2,000AD, why, it's a marriage made in heaven. His Dome is also built in ¹⁄₁₀-scale, but cost much less than one tenth of the original.

Their life span is designed to be the same, which means that in a few years, Len's Dome will blow away, leaving his Stonehenge to stand for another 4,000 years.

"It was so obvious. One had to go with the other."

SHIPBUILDING

The good ship 'Linda Rose' is modelled after the 'Dodo', which used to sail on Lake Windermere in summer. Martin saw some photographs of the Dodo and used them to build the Linda Rose. Just some photos. No plans, no nothing. And don't mention kits to Martin: 'People just assemble kits; I actually build boats.' He's a bit worried about the accuracy of the kettle though. 'It boils a spoonful of water in ten seconds. There may not have been a kettle on the original.' I'm sure nobody will mind. Powered by steam, and radio-controlled, the Linda Rose now plies her trade over Martin's local boating pond.

Martin's been building models all his life. 'I built my first boat when I was five. I learned to use a soldering iron when I was ten.' It takes a lifetime to get this good, but Martin is still learning, and still makes mistakes. So what happens if you build one that you don't like? 'The most important thing in my toolkit is a sledgehammer. I batter 'em to death.'

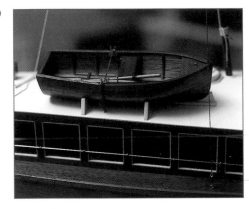

"My wife thinks I'm crackers."

41

NOW THAT'S WHAT I CALL MODELS

Let's face it, we've all made the odd Airfix kit in our time. Geoff here has made 1,283. 'The picture doesn't begin to tell the whole story,' he says. Geoff's flat is rammed with model aircraft, floor to ceiling, and he's expecting the man from the Guinness Book of Records any day.

Of course, they're not all Airfix. As Geoff says, 'Airfix is now a dirty word to me.' They haven't produced a new kit in years. These days, Geoff has to get his kits from specialist shops, and they come from all over – The Czech Republic, Russia, China…

Geoff started when he was nine, while he was recovering from a life-threatening illness, and was encouraged by his family. 'It kept me out of trouble.' And it led to a career – Geoff worked at The RAF Museum in Hendon, where you can see some of his models in the Battle of Britain Hall. A collection like this is the fruit of hours of patient work, a lifetime of research and a lot of sticky fingers.

"It's a real cement; it melts the plastic and welds it together."

ZEN AND THE ART OF HOBBY MODELLING

What great modellers love is the doing of it. The process is more important than the result. Origami is the branch of modelling that embodies process, where modelling is an act of becoming. Origamists recognize that at the heart of the work is the sequence, the steps to be followed. Each step must be relished and understood if the model is going to work.

You could call Origami masters the Jedi Knights of modelling. Nick is Obi Wan Kenobi. Master Nick, he say, 'You take something as commonplace as paper, fold it about for four or five minutes, and make something that people treasure.'

Master Nick thinks it is beautiful and funny. After 20 years of discovering new sequences to fold, Nick gives all his models away. They get soggy overnight. They're not meant to last forever, so why keep them? It was the getting there that was beautiful. As he says, 'The fun is in the folding.'

44

Under his fingers
the white paper crackles. The
crane stretches her wings.

"There are so many origami penguins..."

TRAIN MAN

'25 years ago, I got the hankering to buy an engine,' says Peter. Well, what red-blooded male hasn't felt the same? In the end, Peter bought three full-size industrial saddle tank engines and restored them in his custom-built steam engine shed.

'We're virtually self-sufficient,' he says. 'We've got rivetting gear, the lot. The only thing we have to hire in is a crane.' He runs them too. 'I've got 300 foot of standard-gauge line in the field.' 'Meadow,' says his wife. 'Right, meadow.'

What about the miniatures? 'Oh we just churned those out. Six of 'em. I've got one, the wife's got one. They're based on Hunslet narrow-gauge engines; we run 'em on 7¼-gauge track. You sit behind them, and go round on the track. Great fun. That's laid in the field, 'n' all.' 'Meadow,' says the wife. 'Oh, right. Meadow.'

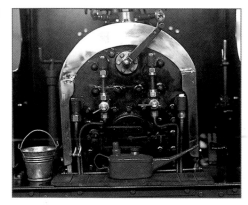

"My wife's involved up to her neck."

AN EVERYDAY TALE OF COUNTRY FOLK

In the idyllic village of Long Lee, you'll find an ancient church with leaded windows casting a warm glow over the churchyard; a village school where apple-cheeked children gambol in the playground; The Druids Arms where honest country folk quaff pints of nut brown ale; four village shops where they always have time to stand and chat; and a farm where many of the honest country folk work. A shame it's not real.

'I'm doing a garage, now,' says Long Lee's creator, Brian. 'It's all made from Yorkshire stone. I chip it up, and grind it up, and then I build with it.' He started a couple of years back, 'just for something to do,' and, as he says, 'it really took off.'

Now people stop by every day to look at the village in his garden; visitors from America have videoed it to show the folks back home, and as for Brian's grandchildren, 'they don't want to go home'. Life looks good in Long Lee.

"I used bits of clay for bananas."

GEORGE AND THE DREAMBOAT

George had a dream. He dreamed of sailing a paper boat down the River Thames. He had not seen himself as a yachting type until the dream, had never really been interested in boats. But dreams have the power to move men and George is English, so salt runs in his veins: Drake, Nelson, George...

'Paper Dream', the world's first papier mâché boat took George six months to build. Then he sailed her 46 miles down the River Thames, through 15 locks, from Oxford to Henley. She came through without a scratch. Without a tear, even. But then George took her on 'The Big Breakfast', where she was treated less than gently, and badly damaged being launched into the canal.

So, the dream fulfilled and a lot of money raised for charity, George burnt her, as Vikings did with their long ships. An honourable death for an elegant lady. Bon voyage, George. May dreams fill your sails.

"I'd like to build another paper boat, and this time I'd like to cross the English Channel."

IF THE CHINESE GO INTO SPACE...

...we'll know who to turn to. Retirement loomed for Frank, and he knew that he needed something to occupy his mind. He started to learn Chinese, but that wasn't enough, somehow, so he became interested in space. Where you or I might read a book or wander outside after the pubs have shut and stare at the stars, Frank began a rigorous training programme. He took all the exams to become a fully-fledged Radio Ham, so he could listen in on the astronauts on the International Space Station as it passed overhead.

Then Frank wondered, what are the processes that go into building a space station? Thus, in order to follow the progress of the work in space, he built a model of it, to better aid his understanding. It's made from old bottles, and bits and bats from about the house, but Frank is pleased with the result. 'I saw another model in the Space Museum in Leicester. I was pleased that mine came so close.'

Oh, and he's still learning Chinese, by the way.

"I check it coming over my house."

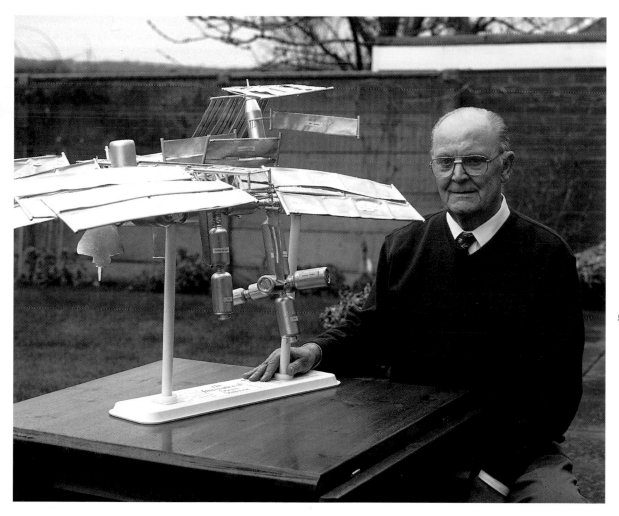

53

THINGS THAT MAKE YOU GO... OOH!

Fred calls them kinetic models. They have a taste of Henry Moore, a drop of Buckminster Fuller (the man who gave the world geodesic domes) and a lot of Fred. He started making them as a college project. Some of his tutors thought he was mad; others, that he was a genius. Fred still can't decide himself.

'The hardest question is when people ask me, "What are they for?"'
So what are they for, Fred? 'You pull them, or push them, and they end up transformed in unexpected ways.'
So what are they for, Fred? 'They are not single objects. They are a series of things.'
Yes, but Fred, what are they for? 'I'm trying to think... They are things. Things! They're not for anything.'

I don't know what they're for, either. I do know that they are beautiful. All I know is I want one, whatever they are for. Fred... can I have one? Please, Fred... can I? Ooh!

"You need to look again, and re-evaluate."

'WE'VE GOT IT OUT NOW'

Modellers are hardy types, out in all weathers in their sheds and workshops, with nothing but a blow-torch for warmth. But when Robert began building his dragster, five years ago, it was during a particularly cold snap, and so he decided to make a start in his kitchen. 'I usually eat out, and I've only got a microwave in there, so it didn't worry me too much.'

When Robert finished building the chassis, he thought that he might still just be able to get the thing out of his kitchen. 'It's like a full-size Airfix kit. You have to get all the bits from America, and it just crept up on me. It's quite good, the sound of a V8 engine running in your kitchen.'

With welding kit running off the ring main for the cooker, Robert built his dragster, which he is hoping to race at Santa Pod. And when it was ready, he knocked down the wall and drove her out. As Robert says, a wall is a lot simpler to replace than a dragster.

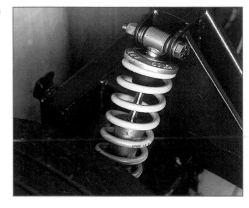

"It's been quite awkward, really."

THE INCREDIBLE SHRINKING MODELS

'I wanted to carry on my profession in miniature,' says Peter. Peter was a building designer in his working life, and now he and his wife have built a dozen model buildings, in the most remarkable detail. They don't just build cinemas, although they do seem to specialize somewhat. As well as The Coventry Hippodrome, they've done The Regal in Leamington and in Minehead, and The Playhouse in Beverley.

But now it gets weird. They made models of all their models, and made a model of The Orangery, the conservatory of a local stately home, which they'd always fancied as a museum to hold their models. So then they put their model models into the model Orangery. This model Orangery contains a model of itself, since it was built to house models of all the models.

Does this model Orangery contain even tinier models? Models of models of models? Peter just laughs. This could go on forever.

"We're all going the same way."

RODOLFO AND THE BLUENOSE

The Bluenose was a Canadian fishing schooner. Between 1921, when she was launched, and 1946, when she sank off the coast of Haiti, she became a Canadian national heroine. She won the International Fisherman's Trophy races five times, and she still appears on the Canadian 10c piece.

Rodolfo fell in love with the beauty of her lines many, many years ago, and vowed that one day he would build a model of her. But although he had built a dozen or so model boats, the time never seemed right to build The Bluenose. She would need too much energy, too much dedication to get right. Rodolfo did not want to rush at it.

Eventually, the time came. As Rodolfo says: 'I find I build better at 60, with worse eyesight, and shakier hands, than I did at 18. One takes more time. One has more dedication, and puts more love into the work. I was in no hurry to finish it.'

"I love to share the bits that I know."

FIVE... FOUR... THREE... THREE AND A HALF...

'There is a huge space race on,' says Richard – no longer between the Russians and Americans, but between various amateur rocketry groups, all aiming to be the first into space. Richard's rockets are already getting up to 10,000–15,000 feet, and he's involved in a group that launches from the Nevada Desert, getting rockets as high as 34,000 feet.

Richard used to work in the space industry, but now his rocketry takes a more modest turn, as in his ½-scale model of a Patriot. There are rocket shops, where you can buy the bits to make your own ground-to-air missile. Amateur rockets are expensive to build, but they have parachutes in them, and, if the builders are lucky, the rockets fall back to earth and they can reclaim all the bits.

So if the nose cone of a large rocket falls through your greenhouse roof, don't panic, Richard will be along in a minute to pick it up.

"I'd like my own asteroid mining company."

'ALL MY DRAGONS COME OUT OF MY HEAD'

The first one came when his daughter got sick, and sighed, and said that she'd love a dragon. So Peter made her one, out of Plasticine – its complexion that muddy, mixed-up colour that Plasticine gets after the kids have been at it.

Since then, the dragons have never stopped coming, some as long as 25 feet. There are dancing Chinese ones, proud Welsh ones – a city of dragons. He builds them from polymers, clays, porcelain, terracotta, concrete and steel. But mostly, he builds them from love.

Dragons, Pete feels, are misunderstood. 'I try to incorporate a little bit of dopiness,' he says of his creations. 'I'd like to build a noble dragon on the Welsh side of the Severn Bridge. I'd like to go around and put them about the country, on a dragon walk, or a dragon hunt.' Or a dragon chase, even.

"If you have an open mind and an open heart, dragons will come to you."

IF BEECHING HAD CLIPPERS INSTEAD OF AN AXE

Mick grew up in this house. It used to be a station. Mick's father worked on the railways, and the house came with the job. Then Beeching closed the line, sometime in the '60s, so there were no trains there any more.

Well, not until old Mick got going. Now you have a steam locomotive, clipped with loving care, and not just any old locomotive, but an 0-8-0 London North Western Railway Super-D. They were used for heavy freight: you need a fair bit of hedge to make something that big.

It takes a bit of upkeep. 'You have to clip it four times a year. And then you have to go out there and snip bits off every week in the growing season. It's a bit of a tourist attraction, my old hedge. I had a bloke come and knock on my door. "I've come a long way to see this hedge," he said. So you can't let it go. You've got to keep clipping. But it's worth it. It goes with the house.'

"I went to town on it."

LIKE THE CIRCLES THAT YOU FIND...

Some models are tiny. And some are 30 feet high, like this recreation of a traditional Sussex smock windmill. Some models don't do much, other than sit about in display cases. Some models, however, generate electricity: enough, eventually, to run Tony's horse rescue centre, and even to sell a little to the National Grid.

Some people don't like the idea of giant windfarms springing up next door, but everyone likes a nice old-fashioned windmill. Tony disguised his generator, so people would think it was pretty.

Some people say that it's not efficient. It's built from old bed posts and the main axle from a Post Office van. It cost six grand. A high-tech wind turbine costs hundreds of thousands, and costs more energy to build than it will ever generate. This is a beautiful model, an example of what human-scale technology is all about. Some people want a clip round the ear.

"You learn to become independent when you're at sea."

THE MESSAGE IS IN THE MEDIUM

Dennis isn't making that many ships in bottles at the present time. He's made over 50, and these days the challenge is beginning to wear off. After all, as he says, 'There's only one way to get them in, there's only one way to get the masts up.'

He began making them one afternoon back in 1966. He was round at his brother-in-law's house, and there was only some boring old football match on TV – England versus Germany, or something – and Dennis was at a loose end while his family watched the game. He looked at a model ship on his brother-in-law's mantlepiece and thought to himself the rigging wasn't right. He thought he could do better, so he had a go.

But he's got the knack of them now. They only take 14½ hours each. So now Dennis is looking for something a bit more challenging. He has begun carving in wood the history of life on this planet over the course of 250 million years. That should keep him occupied, next time there's only the World Cup Final on TV.

"It's time that I'm interested in."

TANK BLOKE

'You may wonder why I always build German things,' Peter asks. The reason comes down to this: the Nazis were mad. The Russians only built one kind of tank, and the Americans just went with the Sherman. This means that, although they might have been rough, they were much easier to maintain and use in battle. But the Nazis, being mad, kept coming up with exotic tanks and armoured vehicles, which were beautifully engineered, technically advanced, and just too elaborate and fancy for their own good.

This makes German tanks a paradise for modellers, according to Peter. His ambition is to produce as many different types as possible. He's sticking to ⅙-scale now – the scale, you may note, of Action Man. 'In the past, I dabbled in all scales.' He built five ¼-scale tanks, a ½-size Tiger, and here he leans nonchalantly on his full-scale half-track armoured vehicle.

⅙-scale is much easier to transport. And is less likely to scare the neighbours, I would imagine.

"I went through the steam period."

I NEVER KNEW IT COULD BE SO... PROFESSIONAL

Phil makes models for a living. Some of his models may seem familiar, like the cactus covered in ice, which was used in a well known car advert, or the hair brush with only a handful of bristles, which was used to sell a hair restorer. 'The Trojan horse was fun. It's made from lolly sticks instead of smelly chemicals, which I use a lot of the time. That one was for a car advert, too.'

What was the strangest thing you've ever had to make? 'That would be jockey shorts with a hidden shelf for storing plastic ice-cubes. The worst bit was loading the ice-cubes while the male model had the shorts on.'

He used to make kits as a lad, and went off to do a design degree. 'These days, you can do a degree in model-making – it's not the sort of thing they tell you at school that you can make a living from.' But like all the modellers in this book, Phil puts his heart and soul into what he does, as well as his head. It's in the instruction booklet: build with love.

"The fun bit is the problem solving."

5

ZING ZING ZING WENT MY HEARTSTRINGS

Reg is, by his own admission, 'a mad fanatic tram and bus enthusiast.' He likes trams best. 'Trams are my love. I'd have loved to be a tram driver,' says a wistful Reg. He went to Russia, just as the Iron Curtain came down, to visit the newly liberated trams. And like lots of tram enthusiasts at the moment, he's feeling a bit smug: 'They're the thing of the future.'

He'd made trams before; this time he wanted to make a bus, and so he spent four years building this old London Transport Scooter Bus in his kitchen. He didn't use plans, just old photos, but as Reg says, 'Whatever's in the original is in mine.'

When he'd finished, however, there was a slight problem. The model was too big to get out of the door, so it had to come out the window. Even then, they had to take the frame out. 'Don't tell the council,' said Reg. I promise, Reg, not a word.

"I had a lovely time round the depot."

A SMOKER'S SMOKER

Ron smokes like a trooper, so he says, but it takes a special kind of smoker to use up 161,000 matches. And then to take those matches and build a model of the Houses of Parliament, floodlit at night, with all four sides of the clock tower working.

It's not easy to build a model of the Houses of Parliament because you can't get hold of plans of the thing, in case a latter-day Guy Fawkes wants to know the best place to hide some dynamite. So Ron used photographs and, after two and a half years, it was finished.

What now? 'I've had four MPs come and visit. They are trying to get a case made, and then its going to be on show in the Palace of Westminster. Wouldn't that be something? And now I'm building an 8-foot long Flying Scotsman. That'll be the biggie.' The problem is, Ron's doctor is urging him to give up smoking, to try the patches. What can you make out of them?

"Silly boys, aren't we?"

SAVING TINY LIVES

Here's David, and his nesting boats. Like a Russian doll, the little one nestles up inside the big one. The back of the main boat drops down and out comes the little one, which is based on German lifeboat used for inshore rescues.

They are both radio-controlled and, as far as David is aware, the tiddler is the smallest radio-controlled boat there is; certainly, he's never come across a smaller one. David makes them from kits (which cost not very much) and then customises them using state-of-the art radio control gear (which costs a great deal).

But when you've built the things, what then? You enter competitions. David is a champion tug tower: his colleague has a 6-foot long model of a super-tanker; David has a model of a high-powered tug. They go to competitions and tug the super-tanker around a floating obstacle course. Together, they're national champions. This would make an ideal TV series, surely: 'One Man and his Tug?'

"I can use the sink and the bath anytime I want."

ROBOP: THE ROBOTIC BIRD OF PREY

Did you know what a problem birds are? Massively so, apparently. Bob is an expert in these matters. 'If you've got a flat factory roof, 1,000 gulls perching on it, that's an awful lot of... em... guano blocking your gutters, and potentially flooding your factory. And landfill sites are a nightmare, trying to keep gulls off.'

The answer is ROBOP, or so Bob and his partner Allan hope. 'It's a Peregrine Falcon. Everything is scared of peregrines,' says Bob, left. Bob modelled the original from polystyrene, though now it's gone into production, it's moulded from aviation-quality fibre glass. Allan puts in the electronics, which mean that ROBOP behaves as much like a real peregrine as possible, so that birds don't become habituated to it.

It doesn't fly, of course? 'Oh yes it does – at least, ROBOP 2 does. It will clear a huge landfill site quicker than anything else. As I say, everything's scared of a peregrine.' Not you, though Bob? 'Och no. I speak to it when it's sitting on the front seat.'

"The bird can phone you up, or we can phone the bird."

AMBASSADOR! YOU ARE SPOILING US!

With this tiny train set in one of your old chocolate boxes! A train-set that is just over 5 inches across!

These Fabergé train-sets hidden, not in Easter eggs, but in television sets, or a computer monitor, or the chocolate box, are built by Doug, a retired railwayman, a driver on the old London–Tilbury–Southend line. He started in steam; now his trains are battery-driven. Where once they were the size of whales, now they are Z-gauge, cute as a puppy's paw.

It started with a coffee-table-sized layout, years back. They started to grow on Doug, the tiny trains, and as a result his layouts have grown progressively smaller over time. 'It's a challenge how small you can get them.' Could they get any smaller? Doug thinks not.

'It's impossible even to build them this small, really,' he says, with a trace of pride in his voice.

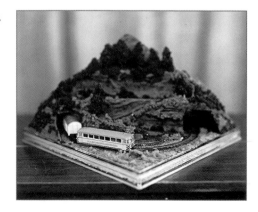

"It's something you can do on your own, indoors, on a table."

THE NEW STEAM AGE

Look at this and wonder. How, you might think, has Peter done this? Has he built a special shrinking machine, gone back in time, shrunk a real steam locomotive and brought it back to the 21st century? No. Hard though it is to believe, Peter built it – every last bit of it.

It's an old Southern Railways 'King Arthur' class locomotive, 'Sir Bors de Gannis'. It's taken four years, so far, and it's still not finished. It only runs on compressed air at the moment, but when it's out on the track and Peter is sitting behind it, it'll run on coal and water.

So what else is left to do? 'Oh, just painting it.' A few days, then? 'Oh no. You have to take it all to pieces to paint it. And then put it all back together again. A few months yet.' No, I think it would be easier to invent the shrinking machine. Quicker too.

"The wife thinks the world of it."

'IT'S JUST A GIFT I'VE GOT'

Love is the most important ingredient, but you need to be full of fire, too. To build models, you need enthusiasm. 'I used to do just the water colours. Oh yes. But then, when that boat got washed up on Brighton Beach... what was it... the Athena B, I thought, oh, I've got to have a crack at that. So I did and I put it in to the Dartford Show, walked away with first prize at the first attempt. Yes. I don't use kits. I use the recycled cardboard, and the balsa wood. To make it stronger. I use the plywood sometimes...'

'...And I've used dowelling rods. No kits. I just gather what I need before I start. I go right from the beginning and right to the finish. I don't do all bridges. I can go from bridges to anything. I've done a lot in London of the famous buildings and bridges there. I've done The Palladium. I've done The Millennium Bridge. I do it from postcards, but I gather all the history, I get in touch with various people, I even go and have a look for myself. Oh, yes. All I've told you, and all I've done is true, and if something new comes out, I'll have a crack at that...' Here's to Frank: model maker, watercolourist, song and dance man. An enthusiast.

"I can even do it again and again if I wanted to."

'WHEN IT ALL GOES RIGHT, IT LOOKS BRILLIANT'

So says Russell (fourth from left), the Busby Berkeley of the world's only radio-controlled model wet-bike formation display team, The Sedgemoor Seajets. To the sound of the theme from Hawaii–Five-O, the eight Seajets come dancing across the boating pond. They do stunts, they do pirouettes, they do crossovers. One of the Seajets has been especially adapted so that it can jump over the others, and two of the drivers can do handstands. All the models are built from kits by their operators.

'It only takes three or four nights to build them,' says Russell, 'but it takes hours of rehearsal to get it right. Luckily, we're all pretty handy with a radio-controller.' A display can only last for 20 minutes, max. 'Two displays in an afternoon, and our batteries are knackered.' And it isn't always easy to get the team together; at the moment they average four performances a year. And four performances mean a great deal of practice, especially when Russell has changed the routine. Catch them, if you are very lucky, at a boating pond near you.

"All the helmets are colour co-ordinated."

FRANK'S CRAFTY CAFÉ PLAN

Frank was opening a café and was worried it would be empty. So he decided to buy a couple of old mannequins and put them in the café to make people would think that there was someone in there. He asked everyone, but nobody seemed to know of any.

Then the phones started to ring, and mannequins came in from all over. Frank found himself in possession of 30, having only needed two, for the opening of his café. His house was full. 'It's them or me,' said Frank's wife. He broadcast an appeal, and the phones started to ring again. This time it was museums, needing mannequins for dioramas. All but one and a half had gone, and peace returned to the house.

Er... But then the phones started ringing again. More mannequins to be rid of. 'People don't like to destroy them,' says Frank. 'It's as though they have some voodoo about them.' Frank can't resist, so the house is full again. Oh, the café is a great success, by the way. Frank didn't need mannequins to lure people in at all.

"The world we live in is not at all funny."

ACKNOWLEDGEMENTS

The author would like to thank:
Chas Ambler; Ian Dicken; Andrew Duplock; Graham Fisher; Peter French; Tony Golding; Paul Hazel; David Hibling; Richard Jones; Andrew Lievens; Bob Machin; Steven Moger; Nik Morrell; Martin Norris; Saleel Nurbhai; Richard Parker; Rikki Patton; Richard Salmon; Nic Shelley; Geoff and Graham Southgate; David Stonestreet; David Westmore; Ian Whiteley; Paul Williams; Ian Willson; Jeff Woodman and everyone else I've ever played with.

For help with research, thanks go to the following individuals and organisations:
Mark Avery (Model Soldier Magazine); Peter Apps (www.sheppey.free-online.co.uk); Jack Bennett; Kat Berry; Hannah Blake; Chris Bland (Large Model Association); Sophie Bomont; Dennis Booker; Philip Burnell; Geoff Byman (FiveO models/GBP Imaging); Paul Crouch; Charles Darley; Fred Dibnah; Chris Donoghue; Claire Downing (British Railway Modelling Magazine); Nigel Elworthy (British Origami Society); Malcolm Franks; Louise Green; Simon Hardman (Ribble Valley Model Soaring Association); Paul Harrington; Stuart Humphreys (UK Tank Club); Elizabeth Jackson (Yorkshire Miniaturists Association); Marianne Jones (Norbury and South London Transport Club); Derek Jones; Susan Jones; David Lane; Rob Lee (Sheffield & District Model Helicopter Club); Tony Little (Model Soldier Magazine); Jason Lythgoe; Alan Marshall; Claire Middear; Metro Models; Sinead Murphy; Niall O'Kane; Bob Orr; Nicola Pike; Albert Raiper; Michael Riley; David Semper; The Sheerness Times Guardian; Leon Smith; Barry Stevens (The South West Association of Model Boat Collectors); Siöbhan Tjübut; Kevin Wilson; Philip Warren.

All the modellers featured can be contacted through the publishers.